GW01395976

101
TINY CHANGES TO
BRIGHTEN YOUR WORLD

101
TINY CHANGES TO
BRIGHTEN YOUR WORLD

AILBHE MALONE

ILLUSTRATED BY BECKY BARNICOAT

ICON

Published in the UK and USA in 2019 by
Icon Books Ltd, Omnibus Business Centre,
39–41 North Road, London N7 9DP
email: info@iconbooks.com
www.iconbooks.com

Sold in the UK, Europe and Asia by
Faber & Faber Ltd, Bloomsbury House,
74–77 Great Russell Street,
London WC1B 3DA or their agents

Distributed in the UK, Europe and Asia by
Grantham Book Services
Trent Road, Grantham NG31 7XQ

Distributed in the USA by
Publishers Group West,
1700 Fourth Street, Berkeley, CA 94710

Distributed in Australia and New Zealand by
Allen & Unwin Pty Ltd,
PO Box 8500, 83 Alexander Street,
Crows Nest, NSW 2065

Distributed in India by
Penguin Books India,
7th Floor, Infinity Tower – C, DLF Cyber City,
Gurgaon 122002, Haryana

Distributed in South Africa by
Jonathan Ball, Office B4, The District,
41 Sir Lowry Road, Woodstock 7925

ISBN: 978-178578-572-6

Text copyright © 2019 Ailbhe Malone
Illustrations copyright © 2019 Becky Barnicoat

The author and illustrator have asserted their moral rights

No part of this book may be reproduced in any form, or by any
means, without prior permission in writing from the publisher

Typeset in Parango OT by Marie Doherty

Printed and bound in Great Britain
by Clays Ltd, Elcograf S.p.A.

CONTENTS

ABOUT THE AUTHOR

Ailbhe Malone is a freelance journalist, a former founding member of *BuzzFeed* UK and its Lifestyle Editor. She has consulted on Lifestyle for *BuzzFeed* internationally and has featured as an industry expert on BBC's *The Apprentice* and for Phaidon's *Where to Eat Pizza* (2016). She has worked for *Nylon* (US), the *Guardian* (UK), *Heat* and *Wired*.

INTRODUCTION

Hello! If you're a first-time reader, welcome. If you're reading this book because you read my first book, *101 Tiny Changes to Brighten Your Day*, welcome back.

Lots has changed in my life since I wrote my first book. I got married! I published a book! I lost my job! I wrote a second book! My anxiety, however, did not change. I still spent the morning of my wedding in the bathroom, doubled over with anxious stomach pains at the thought of everyone seeing me and how I might let them down. I still felt like a massive imposter when I published my first book, and probably did it a disservice by saying: 'Oh, it's non-fiction, just a gift book on self-care.' And I still struggled with trying to be open about my mental health in a way that was authentic to me but that also wasn't *too* open.

What did change though, was how I reacted to my anxiety. With the help of a therapist, I've gotten a lot better at noticing how my anxiety is presenting itself and at sitting with it, rather than allowing it to overwhelm me. For example, my body was freaking out on my wedding morning, but in my head I could say: 'Ah, OK, obviously you are nervous! It is normal to be nervous!' When I found out that my department at work was being cut and I was going to be made redundant, I began trying to plan all the ways I could control the outcome. I would have a job within a month, maximum. I would also use the time off to go to the gym lots and maybe travel to see friends abroad. I consumed myself with these plans and attempts to control what was happening to me, before I realised that I wasn't allowing myself to actually feel anything. I had put so much value on who I was in relation to my job that I didn't want to think about who I would be without that work. I had to start thinking more externally than internally.

The first book focused on how to use self-care to look after yourself, to treat yourself like a friend. **In this book, I want to explore how self-care can be outward-facing**: self-care can mean examining how you interact with the world around you. It can mean advocating for yourself at work and examining how you thrive in different spaces. It can mean taking pleasure in the natural world, and also taking responsibility for the environmental impact you make on the planet. It can mean having difficult conversations with family members, in a thoughtful and supportive way. It can also mean examining relationships with people who don't support you, or who make you feel bad about the way you live your life.

All of this is to say that change never happens all at once. You don't make a birthday cake by putting two already-cooked sponges in the oven. Process, and thoughtful activity, is what leads to real change. Think of it this way: my friend Jeanne posted on her Instagram the other day: 'I was running late for something, but remained on the bus instead of taking a taxi and it was fine, even though I was seven minutes late. Had a veggie-ish dinner. Didn't internet shop on payday!' Her post is a great reminder to be proud of yourself for making an effort – **small changes add up, no matter how tiny**.

These concerns are generalised based on my experiences as a cisgender white woman – I'm under no illusions that if you're LGBTQ+ or a person of colour you have other things to deal with instead of, or in addition to, these things. I've tried to include resources here about how to support friends and family members who will be experiencing a different set of difficulties, working within a system that doesn't support them and that expects, but fails to reward, their labour.

As ever, **take the tips in this book as suggestions rather than rules.** If my experiences differ from yours, or if the tips don't feel right for you, then scribble them out and write your own alternatives in their place. Self-care is about what's right for *you*, and the best person to decide what that means is, well, you.

HOW TO BRIGHTEN YOUR FRIENDSHIPS

This chapter will help you nurture your friendships and be a better friend to yourself.

I've always found it easy to make friends and to keep friendships alive – at least, that's what I'd always believed. But as I've grown older, and my close friends no longer live in the same city as me, I've had to learn how to nurture friendships that don't involve a ten-minute bus ride to watch TV. At university, my favourite thing was how all my friends lived in each other's pockets. We even copied out each other's class timetables so we'd always know who was around for a coffee or some nourishing 11am chips in the canteen. Even in my early twenties, most of my friends stayed in those pockets – I could practically ping-pong around the city and check off seeing my friends, catching up and fuelling our relationships. But as people move out of cities and back to their hometowns, and jobs become more important, it's tricky to feel like you're still getting quality time.

If you're in this situation and you hold on to all of your worries, questions and pieces of news for when you see your friends IRL, you miss out on a lot in between. So, a lot of the tips in this section look at the ways you can nurture friendship from a distance.

Catching up in person is wonderful but can bring challenges too. For instance, my girlfriends and I had a weekend away in Edinburgh the other year, and it was the most fun I've had in a long time. But I still had to push down my fears that nobody would want to spend an extended amount of time with me and that all my ideas for activities were bad (for example, a wet and windy hike). But really, so what if they were bad? It's OK for one friend to enjoy hiking and the other to prefer to check out local coffee shops. There's no way to 'get things wrong'. Maybe, like me, you really value time to chat and catch up in a cosy setting – eating crisps on the sofa is the ideal Saturday night. It takes courage to ask for that from your friends, to say: 'I know there's a great DJ playing tonight, but I'd really like to catch up over a pizza.' I'm proud of myself for asking for what I want – and in doing so, I think I've helped my friends to ask for what they want too. It feels like a gift to be able to let your friendships grow and change.

This chapter will help you nurture your friendships in the same way, but will also encourage you to check in on friendships that maybe aren't serving you as well as they could. Change is OK, and there's no need to fear people changing over time – you've changed too! But like a tree, while leaves may drop off and new buds may form, the trunk of your friendship will always stay firm and rooted in the ground.

/

Make sure you and your
friend have the same
expectations of each other
and set them out clearly.

For example, if you have a friend
who loves to text you their every
waking thought, but you're not great
at texting back, let them know. Say:
'Hey, I'm not great at responding to
text messages, but I see them, and
I'm glad you're thinking of me.'

2

Ask your friends how they want to be supported.

Here's a template for that conversation: 'You mentioned things are really difficult for you at work at the moment, and I want to be there for you. What kind of things can I do to support you through this? What works best for you?'

3

If you find making plans
together difficult, try using a
scheduling site like Doodle or
Calendly. Everybody inputs
their availability across a
range of dates and the site
will find the date that works
for everyone – without lots
of back-and-forth texting.

4

If you find phones are getting
in the way of IRL interaction,
play this game when you go
out for dinner – everyone puts
their phone in the centre of
the table and the first person
to react to a notification
has to pay the whole bill.

5

One of my favourite ways to support my friends is to be very practical. For example, when friends are going through a hard time (whether that's illness or death in the family), I'll drop over with a lasagne or shepherd's pie. I also drop over a meal to friends who have just had a baby – and I have never seen such gratitude as when I turn up, put dinner in their fridge, and tell them I'll come over and chat when they're less exhausted. When trying this out, here are some things to consider: text in advance to check their dietary preferences; make it clear that you won't stay and chat if they don't want to; and make the dish big enough for a couple of servings.

6

If you can't take some
food to a friend in person,
you could gift them a
voucher to a recipe box
service like HelloFresh.

7

Believe your friend when they share their experiences. As Rachel W. Miller writes on *BuzzFeed*:

If they tell you about a personal experience, avoid interrogating them or taking the devil's advocate position. (The devil doesn't need more advocates!!!) Become known as the friend who says, 'I believe you.'[1]

8

It's OK to have only one or two close friends.

Don't worry about other people's #squads on Instagram or try to compare your fearless duo or trio to them. What feels real and right to you *is* real and right.

9

The hardest bit about long-term
friendship groups is that
sometimes one friend will
drift away from you or from
one of the others. If you found
their friendship toxic, it's
OK to say to the others: 'I'm
really happy that this person
is doing well, but I don't really
want to talk about them.'

10

Establish friendship rituals.

———

Every year on the first day of spring
my friends and I have a lunch
together where we exchange presents.
It's my favourite day of the year.

HAPPY SPRING

//

Or carve out specific
and meaningful time
together in another
way – like going to the
theatre regularly with
one friend or having
a group of friends you
do pub quizzes with.

12

If your friendship lives by the group chat, and a friend is going through a complicated and stressful time, you're not a bad friend for asking for a reminder on the situation. Your friend will be happier that you confirm: 'So, James is the brother in this scenario', rather than you asking 'Hang on, who is James?' each time. Be upfront about what you need clarity on, but don't get too bogged down in the details – you don't need to understand every part of what's going on.

13

If you experience anxiety about your friendships and worry that they all hate you (like I do), try to imagine your lovely friends actually saying those horrible words. Doesn't seem likely, does it?

14

If you accidentally
send someone a text
message that was about
them and wasn't meant
for them, apologise. I
have done this. It isn't
great. Just say sorry.

15

Facebook gets a bad rap, but I find it great for talking to faraway friends and family. Don't feel bad if you rely on social media to keep in touch – some of my best chats have been via Instagram DM.

16

Be sensitive towards friends and loved ones who may have a difficult relationship with their family, and welcome them into yours if you can. For example, if Mother's Day is difficult for a loved one, text them to let them know you're thinking of them.

HOW TO BRIGHTEN YOUR WORKDAY

These tips will help you find your
groove at work and introduce
some more balance to your day.

I've been working since I was fourteen – inspired by Anne M. Martin, I started an actual babysitters club. I've worked in delis, as a dental nurse, a cleaner, and a trainee ear-piercer in Claire's Accessories. I've worked in the media for over ten years, as a freelance journalist, a manager at a startup, an editor, and more. I'm someone who took pride in being driven – someone who always had a job, even during a recession.

I recognise that being 'driven' only accounts for some part of my success – I had structural support around me, in the form of my parents, a university degree and my privileged white middle-class background. But I still placed a large amount of my self-worth in how well I performed at work, whether that was becoming a national newspaper columnist at the age of 22, or writing a book while holding down a full-time job. But the problem with putting all of you into your career means that when you're made redundant (Hi! That happened to me!), or when your performance doesn't match your compensation (Hi again!), you can take it personally.

Best working practices are specific to the individual – maybe you're someone who enjoys working quietly, or who gains energy from a vibrant workplace. But work-related stress and burnout are a risk to all of us, regardless of our working style. A 2018 report from the Health and Safety Executive found that over half a million workers in Great Britain were suffering from work-related stress, depression or anxiety (new or long-standing) in 2017/18.[2]

After I burned out a few years ago, I realised I had to change the way I approached things. While I've always been good at ignoring work emails at the weekends, I was taking work emotions and stresses home with me, waking up in a cold sweat with fear. I realised that I'm someone who loves structure, so even though freelancing worked for others, it was never going to be a good fit for me. I began to build better boundaries between my work and personal life.

As well as getting better at trusting friends and colleagues with my worries, I also learned to reach out to an online community for my work concerns; sites like Ask a Manager and Facebook groups for industry peers are invaluable. In times of extreme stress I still find myself sinking back into the bad habits of trying to take on too much at once, or feeling personally responsible for a business change that has nothing to do with me. But these changes meant that when I started a new job search, I was able to really interrogate what was important to me in a workplace, and to be confident in how I wanted to approach my working day.

This chapter will share tips for how to bring more balance into your workday, as well as templates for difficult conversations, and processes that will help you advocate better for yourself.

17

If you work in an open-plan office, or somewhere that uses a shared work calendar, block out chunks of time to focus.

For example, Tuesday mornings are typically quiet for me and a good time to catch up on tasks that require more concentration. So, I put two hours of 'do not disturb' time in my calendar so that nobody can grab me. Think about the way your energy flows during the day and when you could use some uninterrupted time. You could even explore this if you work for yourself – could you 'steal' any time for yourself?

18

It's normal to feel concerned after a big change at work – even if it's a change for the better. And it's OK to ask for extra support during a change.

19

Make your workspace feel like home.

———

Research shows that when your desk feels like a place of refuge, it contributes to 'increased cognitive function'. This leads to increased morale and better well-being in the workplace.[3]

20

Use a timer for intense bursts of concentration.

———

The Pomodoro technique focuses on breaking projects down into 25-minute chunks (called 'Pomodoros'). You take a short break after every 25 minutes, and after four Pomodoros, you take a longer break. This technique works best if you're someone who can really focus intensely – less so if, like me, you tend to daydream.[4]

21

Keep your CV updated as you take on new roles. If the role was listed externally, copy and paste the job description straight into your CV. When you go to apply for a new job, you'll have the responsibilities from your old one written out already.

22

Realise that everyone feels awkward and insecure at work.

———

Some people just hide it better! You are absolutely not the only person on your team who feels anxious about their performance, so try not to beat yourself up for feeling this way.

23

Imposter syndrome is more prevalent for people from minority backgrounds, who tend not to be as well supported in the workplace. In *Slay in Your Lane*, Funke Abimbola explains how finding a support system was vital for her career progression as a black woman:

Mentoring is guidance and advice. Sponsoring is someone actively looking for opportunities for you and putting you forward for them. Coaching is actually teaching you the skills: how to influence; how to communicate; how to get by; this is how you should run the meeting and so on.[5]

24

Nobody is automatically good at
having difficult conversations,
so why not make being better
at having them a work goal?
Admitting to finding something
tricky is not a weakness. And
remember, giving feedback
is a skill that will grow the
more you practise it.

25

When giving difficult feedback, focus on the behaviour, not the person.

If you focus on the behaviour, you separate the action from the person, which means the recipient is less likely to feel personally attacked. For more tips on how to do this, check out Courtney Seiter's article 'The Art and Science of Giving and Receiving Criticism at Work'.[6]

26

But it's hard to hear that you've done something wrong. Take a deep breath and try to receive difficult feedback with grace and an open mind. If you take pride in your work, criticism can feel very personal, but recognise that feedback is there to help you grow. If someone tells you a soup needs more salt, they're not criticising you as a person, they're offering feedback on how to get a good end result.

27

When you're getting difficult feedback and feeling stressed about it, take a tip from negotiation expert Natalie Reynolds on how to feel calm and in control:

Breathe – deeply and slowly. Keep a glass of water close by to prevent coughing and dry mouth. Hold onto the arms of your chair to prevent fidgeting and shifting around. Rather than direct eye contact, look at the space just between the other person's eyebrows when addressing them – it can be less intense and is not obvious.[7]

28

Don't be your own worst boss.

In an essay for the zine 'Do What You Want', Laura Snapes encourages you to write a list of the things that you do when you're letting work overtake you.[8]

Keep your list of overwhelm habits handy so you can check in if you notice yourself doing these things. On the list you could also note what helps you calm down.

29

Really consider whether you need to have your work email on your phone.

––––––

Try to interrogate why you feel the need to check work email on days off. If you work somewhere with an 'always on' culture, you might need to be strict in saying: 'I am not going to be checking emails while I am away.' If the company structure doesn't support your need to switch off from time to time, open up a conversation about it with your managers.

30

Rethink your approach to networking.

———

An article in the *Harvard Business Review* explains that there are three kinds of networking: operational, personal and strategic. Operational helps leaders manage their work internally, personal helps leaders in their development and strategic helps leaders consider new business challenges. It basically means that you can 'network' in your current role and also with your peers. For example, a close work friend can help with personal growth, while a senior mentor will be able to help you connect the dots in your role strategically.[9]

31

When it comes to supporting an LGBTQ+ employee, or any colleague whose lived experience differs from yours, you might find it useful to think about this advice from trans studies academic Jacob Hale, suggested in relation to writing about trans:

Approach your topic with a sense of humility. Interrogate your own position. Don't erase our voices. Don't assume that all trans experiences are the same.[10]

32

Don't be afraid to advocate for your needs.

If you find it difficult to do this in person, it's OK to send an email. If I have a stressful meeting coming up (maybe to negotiate a new contract), I like to email in advance with an agenda. Something like: 'Looking forward to speaking on Friday. I'd like to discuss a raise based on my performance in the past year. I'd also like to discuss the benefits at this company and how to align them with industry standards. For example, we currently offer no maternity pay.'

33

If a meeting doesn't go as well as you had hoped, you are totally within your rights to request a follow-up meeting!

You can also do this via email. Here's a template: 'Thanks for meeting. I had some concerns and queries that weren't addressed on Friday. Could we please meet again on XYZ date? Let me know if you need me to prepare anything.'[11]

34

Here's my best piece of work advice. When you're about to take on a new contract, and the interviewer asks you what your salary expectations are, respond with: 'What's your budget?' It is a normal question to ask, and nine out of ten times they will tell you.

35

Just because a project doesn't reach its goals doesn't mean you can't still be proud of it.

––––––

Think about the process and what you've learned. Rites of passage are surprisingly powerful – so, if it helps, write an email to the project thanking it for what it has taught you.[12]

HOW TO BRIGHTEN YOUR FAMILY RELATIONSHIPS

These tips will help you connect with your family, whether they're your biological or chosen family.

I'm lucky to have a good relationship with my immediate family, and a wide network of people who are like family to me. But I'm not going to pretend that these relationships haven't taken a lot of work.

I also have a very large extended family – 30 first cousins at the last count and fifteen aunts and uncles. Growing up surrounded by this many people, I found it difficult to find my place in the pack. I put a lot of pressure on myself to be superlative: if I couldn't win prizes at music competitions like my cousins, then I could get the best exam results, get a summer job first or be the first something, anything. It makes me sad that I put so much pressure on myself, and now as an adult I'm trying to engage critically with these expectations, and enjoy a relationship with my extended family on a more relaxed footing.

Pressure to relate to your family well – to meet their expectations, be 'best friends' with a parent, be the best aunt or uncle, etc. – can be intense. And social media can often amplify these pressures. (Remember that behind every cute Instagram pic of 'parent goals', there's a backstory.) This chapter will give you tips for navigating online as well as offline communication with your family.

Having a good relationship with your parents, or your siblings, is especially difficult! You may rely on patterns of behaviour that worked for you as a child or a teenager but don't serve you now as an adult. Having an 'adult relationship' means relating to them on a different level than you did as a kid – trying to understand their approach to life and how their past has shaped them into the people they are now. Every time I find out more about my parents, or even about my brothers, the love I have for them deepens. When they invite me into their internal world, I feel honoured by their trust in me and by their choice to let me see a more vulnerable side of their personality.

But you may find that your family don't want to engage in this evolution of your relationship. You may find that your views and politics differ, and it can be frightening to think about how different from them you really are. It might also be hard to think about the expectations, both explicit and implicit, that your family have about the way you live your life.

Throughout this chapter I'm going to use 'family' and 'parents' for shorthand, but feel free to sub in 'friends', 'chosen family' or whatever terms describe your situation best. It's OK to want to work on your family relationships, to get to know your parents better as an adult, or to revisit patterns of behaviour that don't work for you anymore. But it's also OK to acknowledge that maybe you won't have a great relationship with your biological family, and your chosen family can perform that role in your life instead. The tips in this chapter are here to be adapted however suits you best.

36

Ask your family questions about their lives before you entered the scene.

―――――――

My friend Roz wrote a list of questions she wishes she had asked her parents before they died. It's not 'What's the family secret?' but personal questions:

How did they feel when they first became pregnant with you? Why did they want children? What was their time at school like? What did they want to do or be when they were young? What have been the happiest moments of their life? What makes them laugh more than anything?[13]

37

If you'd like to preserve the stories and history of your family or community, the organisation Storycorps provides a set of DIY resources that will help you develop a collection of interviews. They've also got a great list of questions to start with such as: *Who has been the kindest to you in your life?*[14]

38

Start a conversation journal.

It's a shared journal between you and a loved one, which you swap back and forth, asking questions or just noting down your thoughts and what's been happening. It can be a great way to stay in touch long-distance, or to give space to difficult questions.[15]

39

If your family struggles to connect at family gatherings, you could try out conversational games. I've heard of many families talking about 'roses and thorns' at the dinner table: the idea is that each person shares one pleasant part of their day and one annoying part of their day. I know it sounds corny, but it could be a good way to get people chatting.

40

Set boundaries.

––––––

I had a family member who would call me at random times throughout the day, requesting long and emotionally draining conversations. Initially I complied, because I thought I was supporting them by listening. But I realised that it was exhausting me. I felt like poor old Laura Linney in *Love Actually*. So, the next time they called, I said: 'I can't do this in the middle of my workday, and I can't be available every evening. But I can keep a slot on Sundays available for you, every week, to speak for as long as you'd like. And if there's anything else you need to say to me, send me an email, and I'll respond in my own time.'

41

If you have a hard time with your family, it can be bolstering to seek out experiences that mirror your own. In *Slay in Your Lane*, the authors speak to musician Laura Mvula who reflects:

I was raised by a mother, aunties and uncles and a father who didn't have the idea of our mental health being something that even exists. There wasn't even a vocabulary in our household ... I do remember being told by my mum when I complained that I was having a panic attack one time to 'Have a bath, have a hot meal, go to your bed.' It's something that is totally alien to her.[16]

42

Share resources with your family that will help them understand where you're coming from.

———

For example, in *Diary of a Drag Queen*, Crystal Rasmussen writes wonderfully about coming out to their parents, discussing being non-binary and asking them to use a 'they' pronoun. If you're thinking of having a similar conversation, you could share the book with your family as a place to begin.

43

Share things with your family that make you think of them.

44

Take the pressure of expectation
off your interactions.

———

Not every family outing or
encounter will be perfect. Maybe
someone will say something
that hurts your feelings. Maybe
you will do something that you
regret. But when has anyone
ever had a totally perfect day?

45

Connect to your family and heritage in other ways too, like through cooking. Gena-mour Barrett writes about how cooking Jamaican food makes her feel closer to her mum and grandmother:

Cooking curry goat for the first time, with only gut instinct as my guide, reminded me of watching my mum and grandmother cook: the very specific alchemy of sprinkling powders and liquids over a steaming pot. I started off reciting my mother's instructions in my head, but as time went on, I found myself improvising, fluid with the knowledge covertly embedded over the years. I remembered the satisfying sizzle of the meat hitting the hot oil. I recognised the potent smell of curry so characteristic of my grandparents' house. It was my first time, but it felt far from foreign.[17]

46

Embrace voice notes.
If your family live in a
different time zone, it can
be hard to schedule phone
calls, but waking up to a
voice note from a loved
one is really comforting.

47

Try watching a TV show or listening to a podcast together.

———

Sometimes it's easier to come together as a family over an external source. You don't all have to be in the same room or even the same city to watch the same TV show or listen to the same podcast. It could be a nice way to keep in touch and start conversations.

48

Think about which
channels of communication
work best for you and
your loved ones.

———

Be flexible with how you
communicate. You might text
your brother but let him know
it's OK to respond to you by
email if he'd prefer. There's no
perfect way to communicate
with your family members.

49

Vent in a safe space!

I love lurking in closed Facebook groups where a community forms around a certain topic (marriage, parenting, etc.) – the group for the podcast Forever35 is great. I find it really bolstering to see the support and thoughtful responses given to the queries posted.

50

Allow your communication to be messy.

———

Accept the giant group chat, and embrace it. A giant aunts/uncles/ cousins group chat that was set up to arrange visiting my gran when she was at the end of her life is now thriving, a year on. Is it chaotic? Absolutely. Is it where I find out about family news first-hand? Totally.

HOW TO BRIGHTEN YOUR (INTERNAL) WORLD

These tips will help you learn
to support yourself.

When I wrote my first book on self-care, I was still learning what that phrase really meant for *me*. On a basic level, when I was having a hard time with my anxiety, it meant that I needed to take care of myself, tend to my internal world with grace and let my happiness bloom slowly like a precious flower. It meant being open to change, but also learning to hold firm to the things that helped me feel stable. But as my sense of self grew sturdier, and as I got a better idea of what 'well' looked for me, I realised that darling buds and blooms were only surface level. I needed to tend to the weeds and brambles in my garden too.

Self-Care Take Two (Self-Care the Sequel: *2 Self 2 Care*) meant that I needed to look at things I had pushed under the rug, whether that was self-esteem or the pressure I placed on myself that often led to burnout.

With the help of a therapist, I interrogated the roots of this pressure and why I always gave the best advice to friends, but would seldom follow it myself. It was hard! It *is* hard! Therapy is like seeing something scary out of the corner of your eye – you'd rather ignore it, but once you notice it, it's all you can see. Then, once you confront whatever it is, it stops being so scary.

Despite all this work (and, after almost three years in weekly therapy, it still feels like work), I still struggle with opening up to people. On the surface, I'm very social, but internally I hold on to the fear that the best person to get the job done is me, because I don't think anyone else would want to help me. At my friend Lynn's book launch, she mentioned how, when she was under time pressure to submit her book, she asked her husband to help her compile the bibliography. My mind was blown. When I was working on my last book, under time pressure, I had stayed up late on Sunday night compiling the bibliography by myself – and then went into work the next morning. It hadn't even occurred to me that I could ask someone for help. Shortly afterwards I was so tired and burned out that I lost my sense of taste.

It's unlikely that you've had the exact same experiences as me, but I'm willing to bet that they'll resonate with you in some way, or that you'll know someone going through something similar. Burnout is prevalent among millennials, and most people can relate to taking on too much – whether that's workload, worries or the woes of others. Maybe you dedicate too much of yourself to your job and find yourself crashing out on the sofa after work every night. Maybe you find it hard to tell friends and family 'no' when you've got too much on your plate.

That's where this chapter comes in. Take this as the first step to listening to what you really want. Take out a pen and highlight any passages that resonate – or scribble through anything that sounds like it's just not for you. This chapter will talk about burnout and self-care, how to check in and make sure you're supporting yourself, and how to let others know how they can support you too.

51

Share different concerns with different people.

Think about whose skills can help you solve the problem. Maybe you have a friend who is good on relationship advice, or a professional mentor who can help you with a tricky topic.

52

Allow your friends to help you.

———

Think of how you support them, and
how much they want to support you.
My friend Catherine once sent me
a message saying that if I wanted
to talk, she would be 'honoured
to listen'. What a thoughtful
way to say 'I'm here for you.'

53

Let go of resentment over others'
happiness with their own timeline
– especially if they achieve a goal
you're working towards, or if their
experiences seem to reflect negatively
on your own. You know what I mean
– maybe a friend from school has just
had a super promotion while you're
figuring out your first career move.
Remember the decisions and positives
that have led to your current situation
and think, with grace and sincerity:
'That's good for you, but it's not where
I am right now, and that's OK.'

54

Recognise that work can be a release, as long as it doesn't take over your life. In an article for *The New York Times*, Anna North writes about the release of losing yourself in work you enjoy:

Chilling out just doesn't work for me the way work does [...] I remember finishing a daylong project in Iowa City last year, ahead of the Iowa caucus, and realizing that all the worries that had entered the city with me had been pushed aside by the voices of the people I talked to, by the process of fitting them all together. To work, for me, is to care for the self by putting the self aside.[18]

55

Find a quiet task that
gives you pleasure.
I'm obsessed with
jigsaw puzzles.

56

Find a 'well': an activity, person or a place that can fill you up when you're feeling empty.

Mental health professional and founder of Muslim Wellness Foundation Kameelah Rashad encourages us to ask ourselves: 'Where do I go to feel nourished and affirmed? To feel understood?'[19]

Maybe it's a YouTube clip of a dog dressed as a dinosaur, or watching your friend's baby discover apple puree. It could be calling your parents, or sitting in the park. Recognise your 'well' and visit it often to draw replenishment.

57

Take control of
your finances.

———

There are plenty of great
resources on personal finance,
but I like @thefinancialdiet on
Instagram, which provides smart
and thoughtful tips for keeping
an eye on your income.

58

You could also try using a money tracking app like Mint, or a debit card like Monzo, to keep a visual marker of how much you're spending and what you're spending it on.

59

Be aware of burnout.

———

Mental health organisation ReachOut provides a simple checklist of warning signs, such as losing motivation or feeling unable to concentrate on tasks. Check it out and think about what warning signs you might need to look out for in yourself.[20]

60

Think about any repetitive
behaviours you enact, and what
they say about your level of stress.

———

For example, I become fixated on
plucking my eyebrows – often to
the point of having cuts on my
forehead from digging in with the
tweezers to get a stubborn hair.
When I notice myself doing that
now, I take a breath and think: 'This
isn't actually about the hair, is it?'

61

Advocate for yourself.

The charity Mind has a useful Wellness Action Plan template. You can use it in the workplace, or even with your friends and family, to write down what mental wellness looks like for you. Having a document that maps out your needs will help bolster you to have tricky conversations and will also help your friends and family check in with you when they see you struggling.[21]

62

If you're feeling overwhelmed,
and you have the resources,
speak to a professional therapist.
Your doctor can refer you, or
there are charities like Mind
or the National Alliance on
Mental Illness which can help
direct you in your choices.

63

Learn to say 'no'.

———

For me, advocating for myself means saying loudly: 'No, I can't do that right now.' Ironically, even when I was writing a book on self-care, I found it hard to leave some fuel in the tank for myself. I still find it very difficult for to say: 'I can't do this, I have too much on right now', but the relief after I do say it is amazing.

64

If you find yourself getting stuck in a pattern, try speaking out loud to yourself.

When I get overwhelmed, I find it helpful to speak out loud to myself, the way a kind teacher or parent would. If I'm feeling annoyed with myself for not achieving as much as I had hoped, I might interrogate that feeling a little, and ask: 'Who set the rules? You did! You've just written 1,000 words about your worst fears – of course you're too tired to write more.'

HOW TO BRIGHTEN YOUR HOME

These tips will help you make your
home a place of refuge and a cosy nest.

When I first started getting treatment for anxiety, I put a lot of thought and effort into making my home feel like a refuge. At the time, there was lot of change in my life – my mum was very sick, my job was very stressful, and I had just bought my first house. Stepping through the front door into a space that felt alien and unhomely was like stepping from a whirlwind into a whirlpool – I craved a space that felt personal and safe.

Now, three years later, my home feels like a haven. I've nurtured the garden and painted the bedroom in calm dark blue. I take lots of pleasure in texture, so there are sheepskin rugs on the floors and velvet throw pillows on the sofa. I love to take care of things, so there are plants everywhere. Every part of my house feels like a gift to myself, a place I've created where I can just take a breath and relax.

I wish I'd known how important a comforting and secure space was to me years ago. When I first moved out of my parents' house, I focused on things that looked right, or trendy, rather than things that brought me pleasure. It was important to me that others viewed my home (and my clothes) as covetable – no matter if it wasn't exactly how I wanted it to be. Even living in shared houses, I didn't realise that I could make my own nest exactly how I wanted it. I wonder how much more settled I might have felt in those early years if I had made a comforting place of retreat for myself.

As I was growing up, I moved around, and when I left home I moved house almost every year. So I'm not sentimental about change. In fact, I'm a demon for a monthly clear-out. But I do agree with Marie Kondo's credo that what you own should 'spark joy'. Let where you live make you as happy as it can.

As ever, it's important to think about budget and access when talking about interiors. Yes, I can write about 'creating a sanctuary', but try not to put too much pressure on yourself to find the *perfect* thing that you spotted on Instagram. Think about texture and comfort as much as you think about aesthetics. There's a reason 'homey' is such a great compliment to receive when someone walks into your house.

On another level, think about what level of cleanliness is right for you, and what is achievable. The goal is to make your home a bright and welcoming place, one that reflects you. Your home doesn't need to live up to anybody else's standards. So, when we talk about clean homes in this chapter, or decorating, mobility issues might mean some tips are not useful for everyone. I've tried to add a note here and there with any substitutions.

65

Stop striving for perfection in your home, and aim for 'good enough'. Don't wait until things are perfect before enjoying where you live.

66

Follow people on Instagram whose homes give you pleasure.

⸺

It could be a family whose house is populated by two giant dogs, or it could be a freelancer who has turned their rented home into a luxurious writing palace. It could also be a popular house cleaning account. What's important is that it reflects how you feel (or want to feel) when you step into your own home.

67

Try the Marie Kondo method – sort through and clear out your belongings on the basis of whether they 'spark joy' or not.

It's a brutal and very effective way of cutting through the bulk, and has worked very well for lots of my friends and colleagues. I'd recommend you follow the book rather than collating tips via articles, because that way you follow a method and learn more about the intentions behind the process.[22]

SPARKS JOY?

68

Clearing out your belongings using the Marie Kondo method might also help you to do an internal clear out too. Sandy Allen explains how Marie Kondo helped them to 'sort out' their gender:

A month later, kneeling and sobbing before my Marie Kondo discard pile, it felt silly, sure, that this book is what had finally done it, but I also couldn't unsee my actual preferences: so much of the feminine clothing I owned did not spark joy. I donated it all. I hung and folded the items that remained: flannel shirts, baggy jeans, t-shirts.[23]

69

It's also OK to keep stuff!

I am probably too keen to throw things away, and my husband often has to say: 'You know, it's OK to be sentimental.' I compromise on this by displaying sentimental items around the house – on my walls I have framed postcards that friends have sent over the years. But I also go through everything once a year and get rid of things that don't speak to me any more.

70

Design your home according to the way you live in it – not the way you'd like to live in it.

If you end up eating most of your dinners on the sofa, why not get some bowls that will let you feast off your lap? If your living room gets chilly, then buy a blanket that can live there eternally instead of going in and out of a cupboard.

71

Clean your home according to the way you live in it too. For example, leave a bottle of shower spray in the corner of the cubicle to rinse it with after each shower. You could even decant the spray into a cute glass bottle (get them on eBay!) so that you don't have to look at obvious cleaning products every day.

72

Think of your home as an 'ecosystem' that nurtures you. In *The Shaping of Us*, Lily Bernheimer writes about how spaces structure our lives, behaviour and well-being. Think about your budget and what is feasible for you. Bernheimer suggests emphasising natural elements like light, nature and 'refuge': 'Consider how you arrange a room in terms of refuge and prospect, craft semi-sheltered nooks, and make the most of natural elements like light and views ... Connect the inside with the outside.'[24]

73

Make your decor do double duty.

———

I like to dry out flowers after they've bloomed and then display them. This double duty can also extend to sentimental items. I dried out the floral centrepiece from my wedding, and now every time I look at the kitchen table I'm reminded of the fun we had.

74

You can find the user guide for absolutely anything online. There is no need for you to hold on to the manual for your toaster.

75

My friend Sophie swears by a ten-minute clean. It's the first thing she does in the evening after coming home from work. Do it before you sit down, and be amazed by what you can get done in ten minutes.

76

Arrange a home items 'swap' with friends.

———

Maybe you've got something you're
sick of but which your friend has had
their eye on for a long time. Maybe
you're planning to throw out a pot
that doesn't fit in your cupboard but
which is perfect for your friend who
loves to make big batches of soup.

77

Set a realistic picture of what 'good enough' is for you.

———

For me, I hate dirty countertops but don't mind clean dishes stacked by the sink. You might be fine with clean laundry piled up on 'the chair', but hate the laundry racks hanging out in the living room. Recognise what bugs you the most and target that.

78

A mattress topper is the perfect investment for any type of home. It will make you feel like you're sleeping on a cloud. Plus, if you're renting, it's easier than a mattress to take with you when you move house.

79

If you're renting, ask your landlord if you can swap out some of the items in the house for things that make it feel more like your own. If you're not able to swap out items, see if anything can be flat-packed and stored away until you move out.

80

Another renting tip: if your landlord doesn't allow you to drill into the walls or to hang up pictures with nails, you could try using Velcro command strips. They're strips that attach to the walls but don't leave a mark when you take them down.

81

If you want to brighten up
your home or office with plants
but you have black thumbs
(as opposed to green fingers),
it's cool to have fake plants,
and they can bring you just
as much succour as real ones.
IKEA has plenty of frondy fake
palms that will do the trick.[25]

82

It's OK to spend money on boring things that make your life better.

___

I once had a big fight with my husband about spending £30 on a kitchen bin, but every time it closes tightly and traps in the pongy rubbish smell, I concede that it was probably worth the money.

83

Make your life as easy as possible – if a change is easy to implement, it's going to be more likely to stick.

For example, I got fed up with crumbs on our sofa whenever we ate dinner there, and splashed £20 on a handheld vacuum cleaner. It is my new obsession, as it means I can clean up instantly and with little effort.[26]

HOW TO BRIGHTEN YOUR WORLD

The tips in this chapter will help you engage with the world around you in a thoughtful way.

When we talk about environmental impact, it can be easy to feel helpless. Or at least, that's how I feel. I get caught in a chain of guilt that starts with 'My holiday flights are killing penguins!' and ends with 'My bacon sandwiches are contributing to climate change, which is contributing to loss of lives!' Large-scale change is overwhelming, and on an individual level it's almost paralysing: where do you start when there are so many changes that need to be made? You might feel a personal obligation to fix the world, one tofu stir fry at a time. (Although whether tofu is the solution is also up for debate!)[27]

It's a push and pull between the personal and the collective, and sometimes it feels like personal efforts have little impact on the collective outcome. But that's not true – a 2008 study found that societal indicators on a personal level had a big impact on collective behaviour. For example, the study discovered that 'people were more likely to litter in a heavily littered environment than a clean one'.[28]

The small changes you make *do* have a big impact. You're probably doing fine, but you could probably also incorporate some smaller changes to improve your contribution.

As always, it's important to think about the abilities and circumstances of others – I'm able bodied and live in a large city, but I *still* find it hard to buy in bulk as I don't own a car. If you manage to bring home a ton of quinoa on the bus in reused jars, then you are my hero. If not, don't feel too bad about it. Don't let striving for perfection stop you from making changes that are manageable for your levels of mobility and access. For instance, there are many reasons why some people need plastic straws, and in the same way, if you have chronic fatigue and find it hard to conceive of making your own cleaning products from vinegar and bicarb, then cleaning wipes are fine! (Increasingly you can buy biodegradable wipes too.) Take a look at the following tips and adapt them in a way that works for you. It's your world, after all.

84

Switch to eco-friendly gas
and electricity suppliers,
like Bulb in the UK or
Invenergy in the US.[29]

85

Explore ways to reduce your personal energy use.

———

For example, use low power mode on your phone or laptop. Using less power will mean they require less electricity to recharge.

86

Reduce your heating by one or two degrees.

———

According to a report from the Department of Energy and Climate Change, this is the household behaviour that reduces the most energy:

The ranking may surprise some readers, because behaviours commonly thought significant are some way down the list. 'Only filling the kettle to the required level', for example, may only save 1 TWh, while 'Washing clothes at 40 degrees or less' may only save 0.4 TWh.[30]

87

Unplug chargers from the
wall when your device
has finished charging.

88

Consider using eco-friendly alternatives to everyday items, like beeswax wraps instead of cling film, and reusable water bottles and coffee cups. If it will motivate you to take one out with you, there are lovely stainless steel water bottles available. But they don't need to be expensive! The point is just to avoid buying single-use bottles and cups wherever possible.

89

Try out meat-free Mondays.[31]

And make it easy on yourself by buying vegetarian ready meals, which can help you to learn new veggie options and will mean you don't fall back on 'easy' meat-based dishes if you're feeling uninspired. I like those from Deliciously Ella, and – as an added bonus – the packaging for the range is fully recyclable.

90

If you don't have the bandwidth
to cook a vegetarian or vegan
meal at home (or don't fancy
cooking three different dinners
for your guests or family),
try it when you're eating
out. I can speak highly of
ordering a veggie rice bowl
at your local burrito place.

91

If you have the means, try to reduce plastic when you shop. Some stores let you bring your own containers which you can fill up directly with pasta or grains.

92

If buying a large amount
of unpackaged groceries
isn't for you, think about
smaller unpackaged
purchases of things
like toiletries. I love the
'naked' skincare range at
Lush – people rave about
their shampoo bars.

93

Make substitutions that fit into your life without requiring you to change your habits, like switching to recycled toilet paper, biodegradable bin bags or bamboo toothbrushes. For example, the company Who Gives A Crap makes toilet paper using recycled paper, and donates 50% of their profits to help build toilets for those in need.[32]

94

Take all the help you can get by looking into energy-saving schemes and subsidies from your local government or private providers. For example, in the UK, Thames Water will supply you with a range of free water-saving gadgets, like a water-efficient shower head.[33]

95

Make choices that align with your ethics, as well as your budget and body, by seeking out second-hand or ethically made clothing. High street brands are making strides in eco-conscious clothing too. Did you know that Primark has a range of gym wear made from recycled polyester? And H&M has a 'conscious' range.

96

When buying clothes, adopt a 'one in, one out' policy.

———

Think of whether your new purchase
will go with what you already
own – or whether you're making
a purchase for the sake of it.

97

If you order a takeaway, add a note to say you don't need plastic cutlery or napkins.

98

If you want to use
your local food waste
recycling but hate the
smell as it sits around
waiting for collection,
you can easily shove your
food compost into the
freezer, then take it out
just before collection.

99

Take old clothes to
a clothes bank.

100

Shove a tote bag or plastic shopping bag in your backpack and never have to pay 5p at the checkout again.

101

Finally, celebrate your achievements, no matter how small.

When I got made redundant from my job, I didn't get a leaving card or a gift. But I bought myself a small present and wrote myself a card saying how proud I was of how much I had achieved in that job. Give yourself the permission to be proud of your work, even if the end result isn't exactly what you had anticipated.

NOTES

1.   Rachel Wilkerson Miller, Anna Borges, Terri Pous and Gyan Yankovich, 'A More or Less Definitive Guide to Showing Up for Friends', *BuzzFeed*, 10 July 2018. https://www.buzzfeed.com/rachelwmiller/the-ultimate-guide-to-showing-up-for-other-people

2.   'Work related stress, depression or anxiety statistics in Great Britain, 2018', Health and Safety Executive Annual Statistics, 31 October 2018. http://www.hse.gov.uk/statistics/causdis/stress.pdf

3.   'Studies indicate that personalisation has many benefits, such as greater satisfaction with work, increased well-being, higher morale and lower staff turnover. These positive psychological benefits are understood to be a result of support for the expression of identity and distinctiveness.' Wells, M., Thelen L. and Ruark, J. (2007), 'Workspace Personalisation and Organisational Culture: Does Your Workspace Reflect You or Your Company?'

quoted in *The Shaping of Us*, Lily Bernheimer (2017) p47.

4.   If you'd like to explore this more, there are some apps that mimic the technique, and https://tomato-timer.com is a website that serves the same function.

5.   *Slay in Your Lane,* p80. (See Reading List)

6.   Courtney Seiter, 'The Art and Science of Giving and Receiving Criticism at Work', *Fast Company*, 12 September 2014. https://www. fastcompany.com/3039412/the-art-science-to-giving-and-receiving-criticism-at-work

7.   *We Have a Deal*, p206. (See Reading List)

8.   'Do What You Want' was a one-off zine edited by Ruby Tandoh and published in 2017. It is now out of print.

9.   Herminia Ibarra and Mark Lee Hunter, 'How Leaders Create and Use Networks', *Harvard Business Review*, January 2007. https://hbr.org/2007/01/how-leaders-create-and-use-networks

10. From Jacob Hale's 'Suggested Rules for Non-Transsexuals Writing about Transsexuals, Transsexuality, Transsexualism, or Trans'. As referenced in Meg-John Barker and Jules Scheele, *Queer: A Graphic History*, Icon, 2016, p144. https://perma.cc/9T6W-8ERX

11. If you want more information on this kind of thing, I really like *We Have a Deal*. (See Reading List)

12. I know this sounds barmy, but this is what Steve Jobs did when he held a mock funeral for an operating system (as recounted in *The Power of Moments*, p35): 'Mac OS 9 was a friend to us all. He worked tirelessly on our behalf, always hosting our applications, never refusing a command, always at our beck and call, except occasionally when he forgot who he was and restarted.'

13. Rossalyn Warren, 'Questions to ask your parents before they die', *Medium*, 13 June 2016. https://medium.com/@rossalynwarren/questions-to-ask-your-parents-before-they-die-14ae89ba9521

14.   StoryCorps provides questions for conversations with different people like colleagues or grandparents, or on topics from religion to ill health: https://storycorps.org/participate/great-questions

15.   Find out more in Karenna Meredith's article, 'My Mom Used a "Conversation Journal" with Me as a Kid, and It Made All the Difference', *PopSugar*, 16 December 2018. https://www.popsugar. co.uk/parenting/Why-Parents-Should-Use-Conversation-Journals-Kids-45604457?

16.   *Slay in Your Lane*, p308. (See Reading List)

17.   Gena-mour Barrett and Fiona Rutherford, 'Sunday Dinner, Jamaican Style', *BuzzFeed*, 23 October 2015. https://www.buzzfeed.com/ genamourbarrett/yuh-jus-haf-fi-use-yuh-eye?utm_term =.pwn3pjemme#.eroYKlk33

18.   Anna North, 'Work Is My Self-Care', *The New York Times*, 21 March 2017. https://www.nytimes. com/2017/03/21/opinion/work-is-my-self-care.html

19.   Kameelah Rashad, interviewed by Sally Tamarkin in '15 Ways Muslims Can Feel Just a Little More OK Right Now', *BuzzFeed*, 2 February 2017. https://www.buzzfeed.com/sallytamarkin/muslim-selfcare?utm_term=.xj0LeJmw2v#.qh8N2Qj1lx

See also Kameelah Rashad's organisation, Muslim Wellness Foundation at: https://muslimwellness.com

20.   Find the symptoms and what you can do about it on the ReachOut website: https://au.reachout.com/articles/burnout-and-chronic-stress

21.   You can download a guide for employees and for managers from Mind: https://www.mind.org.uk/workplace/mental-health-at-work/taking-care-of-your-staff/employer-resources/wellness-action-plan-download

22.   Marie Kondo, *The Life-Changing Magic of Tidying* (Ebury, 2011)

23.   Sandy Allen, 'How Marie Kondo Helped Me Sort Out My Gender', *them*, 26 February 2019. https://www.them.us/story/marie-kondo-gender#intcid=recommendations_default-popular_f18e8417-bb40-4e7f-8112-6937b984790e_cral-top1-1

24.   *The Shaping of Us*, p291. (See Reading List)

25.   Cindy Fulton, 'The Impact of Real and Artificial Plants on the Patient Experience in the Hospital Setting', 2014. *School of Physician Assistant Studies*. Paper 502. https://commons.pacificu.edu/cgi/viewcontent.cgi?article=1470&context=pa

26.   For more on this, read *Atomic Habits* by James Clear, which talks about the importance of making the habits you want to implement easy to do (Random House Business, 2018).

27.   Leo Hickman, 'Is tofu bad for the environment?', *Guardian*, 19 February 2010. https://www.theguardian.com/environment/green-living-blog/2010/feb/15/ask-leo-tofu-bad-for-environment

28.   Noah Goldstein, Robert Cialdini and Vladas Griskevicius, 'A Room with a Viewpoint: Using social norms to motivate environmental conservation in hotels', *Journal of Consumer Research* Vol. 35, No. 3 (October 2008), pp472–82. https://www.jstor.org/stable/10.1086/586910?seq=1#metadata_info_tab_contents

29.   Bulb is still quite a new company, so there are plenty of discount/sign-up codes available. Find out more at: https://bulb.co.uk

30.   Palmer et al., 'How Much Energy Could Be Saved by Making Small Changes to Everyday Household Behaviours?', Cambridge Architectural Research and the Department for Energy and Climate Change, November 2012. https://assets. publishing.service.gov.uk/government/uploads/system/ uploads/attachment_data/file/128720/6923-how-much-energy-could-be-saved-by-making-small-cha.pdf

31.   Oliver Milman, 'Why Eating Less Meat Is the Best Thing You Can Do for the Planet in 2019', *Guardian*, 21 December 2018. https://www. theguardian.com/environment/2018/dec/21/lifestyle-change-eat-less-meat-climate-change

32.   https://uk.whogivesacrap.org

33.   https://watersavingdevices.thameswater.co.uk

READING LIST

These are the handful of books referenced throughout the book. I've tried to choose books written by people from a variety of backgrounds and with a variety of viewpoints to ensure you can find something that will speak to you – or surprise you! You should be able to find them all in your local library.

———

If you want to read up on how your environment impacts your day-to-day life (whether that's at work or at home), then try:

The Shaping of Us by Lily Bernheimer (Robinson, 2017)

The Power of Moments by Chip Heath and Dan Heath (Bantam Press, 2017)

These two books are full of fascinating social psychology but are also good reads in their own right.

———

If you want to read up on how to lead a more eco-friendly life (whether that's small-scale tweaks or big changes), then try:

101 Ways to Go Zero Waste by Kathryn Kellogg
 (Countryman Press, 2019)
Save the World by Louise Bradford
 (Summersdale, 2018)

101 Ways ... is focused on large lifestyle changes, whereas *Save the World* includes smaller tips.

———

If you want to read up on the workplace (whether that's being a leader, advocating for yourself or navigating different environments), then try:

Slay in Your Lane by Yomi Adegoke and
    Elizabeth Uviebinené (4th Estate, 2018)
We Have a Deal by Natalie Reynolds (Icon
    Books, 2016)
Ask a Manager by Alison Green (Piatkus, 2018)

Ask a Manager has some workplace scenarios
that will make you think, 'Wow, people are
wild.'

———

If you want to read up on LGBTQ+
experiences (whether from a personal
standpoint or to support a friend or colleague),
then try:

Diary of a Drag Queen by Crystal Rasmussen
    (Ebury, 2019)
Queer: A Graphic History by Meg-John Barker
    and Jules Scheele (Icon Books, 2016)

Diary of a Drag Queen is laugh-out-loud funny, and *Queer* has a lot on queer theory and the history of the queer movements.

ACKNOWLEDGEMENTS

Thanks to everyone who read, bought, and got in touch with me about my first book – you're the reason I got to write another one! Thanks to Juliet and Hattie for being wonderful agents, Kiera for her kind and firm editing hand, and Becky for agreeing to do the fantastic illustrations. I feel so lucky have such a great team around me.

Thanks to my friends who I've quoted throughout – and to the ones who I didn't quote but couldn't have written this book without. I hope my love for my friends shines through this book, especially my best babes Clare, Hannah, Muireann and Lucie. Thanks Nikki for being my eternal cheerleader.

Thanks to Mum, Dad, Rob and Rory, I lahv you all. Thanks to my extended family, who bought Easons out of copies of my first book. And thanks to my in-laws, who have been my second family for the longest time.

As ever, thanks, Diane, for listening. And thanks, Chris, my sweet otter half, for being number one supporter of Team Ailbhe.

Also available

101
TINY CHANGES
TO BRIGHTEN YOUR DAY
AILBHE MALONE

101 *Tiny Changes to Brighten Your Day* is a friendly book of tips on how to look after yourself and your mental health, in an age where we too often forget to pause and take a breath.

For anyone with anxiety issues, those who struggle to prioritise their own mental health over catching up on emails and social media, or those looking for a bit of encouragement, these small tips will help you shine again.

A totem for your bedside table, backpack, or to give to a friend in need, this book believes that you're worth looking after, even when you don't.

9781785783944
(9781785783951 ebook)